TEC

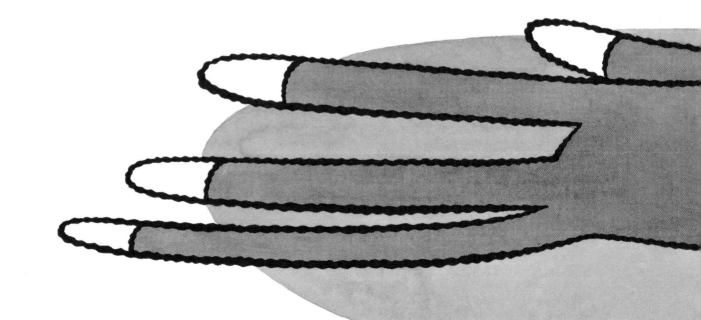

MathStart® COMPARING WEIGHTS

# MIGHTY MADDIE

by Stuart J. Murphy • illustrated by Bernice Lum

HarperCollins Publishers

LEVEL
1

To our very own mighty Maddie
—S.J.M.

for lisa, sarah, jina, julie & nimali . . . many, many thanks
. . . love you guys.
—B.L.

The publisher and author would like to thank
teachers Patricia Chase, Phyllis Goldman, and Patrick Hopfensperger
for their help in making the math in MathStart just right for kids.

HarperCollins®, ▲®, and MathStart® are registered trademarks of HarperCollins Publishers.
For more information about the MathStart series, write to
HarperCollins Children's Books, 1350 Avenue of the Americas, New York, NY 10019,
or visit our website at www.mathstartbooks.com.

Bugs incorporated in the MathStart series design were painted by Jon Buller.

Mighty Maddie
Text copyright © 2004 by Stuart J. Murphy
Illustrations copyright © 2004 by Bernice Lum
Manufactured in China by
South China Printing Company Ltd. All rights reserved.

Library of Congress Cataloging-in-Publication Data
Murphy, Stuart J.
Mighty Maddie / by Stuart J. Murphy ; illustrated by Bernice Lum.—1st ed.
p.  cm. — (MathStart)
"Level 1. Comparing weights."
Summary: As Maddie cleans up her room, she learns how to compare the weights of
various objects.
ISBN 0-06-053159-2 — ISBN 0-06-053161-4 (pbk.)
1. Weight (Physics)—Measurement—Juvenile literature. [1. Weight (Physics)—
Measurement. 2. Measurement. 3. Orderliness. 4. Cleanliness.] I. Lum, Bernice, ill.
II. Title. III. Series.
QC90.6.M87 2004
389'.1—dc22
                                                                                    2003017610

Typography by Elynn Cohen  1 2 3 4 5 6 7 8 9 10  ❖  First Edition

# MIGHTY MADDIE

"Madeline Grace!" said Mom. "Your birthday party starts in two hours. Just look at this house! There are toys everywhere!"

5

Mom was right.

There were toys in the living room,

toys in the kitchen,

6

and toys in the front hallway.

There were even toys in the bathroom.

"Teenie and Jumbo don't have to pick up their toys," said Maddie.

"Dogs and cats don't know any better," said Mom. "But you do. You're a big girl now."

"C'mon, Maddie," said Dad. "I'll help. I'll carry the heavy things up to your room, and you can carry the light things. But then you have to clean up your own bedroom. That's the biggest mess of all."

"I'll take this big box of books," said Dad. "It's so heavy I can hardly lift it."

"These two books are light," said Maddie. "I can carry them."

13

"Your piggy bank is small," said Dad.
"But it must be full because it sure is heavy."

"This pillow is big, but it's very light.
I can handle it," said Maddie proudly.

Before long all of Maddie's toys were in her room. "You have to do the rest, Maddie," said Dad. "Fill up these boxes and bins with your toys and call me when you're finished.

I'll lift them onto your closet shelf—they'll be very heavy for you."

"Boy," said Maddie. "This is one huge mess. It looks like a job for . . . Mighty Maddie!"

"You'd better stay out of the way, Teenie and Jumbo," said Mighty Maddie.

"You're nice and light, Teenie. But you're soooo heavy, Jumbo."

"This dump truck is heavy," groaned Mighty Maddie.

"But this fire truck is even heavier."

22

"My ballerina tutu is very light," she added. "But these feathers are even lighter!"

"Better hurry up, Maddie," Mom called from downstairs. "Your friends will be here any minute!"

Mighty Maddie cleaned up faster than anybody had ever cleaned up before.

"Mom! Dad!" Maddie called. "I'm all done."
Mom and Dad came up to see.

"Amazing," said Dad. "You not only finished in time, but you lifted those boxes and bins with your heavy toys in them all by yourself.

You really are Mighty Maddie!"
Just then the doorbell rang.

"Mighty smart!" said Mighty Maddie.

HAPPY

31

In *Mighty Maddie*, the math concept is comparing weights. For children to understand this concept, they need to have the opportunity to pick up objects and compare their weights. This allows them to observe that the weight of an object is not always dependent on its size.

If you would like to have more fun with the math concepts presented in *Mighty Maddie*, here are a few suggestions:

• Before reading the story, discuss weights with the child. Point out that a large object can weigh less than a small object. The child could hold a pillow in one hand and a can of soup in the other and compare the different weights.

• Gather some of the objects found in the story, like books, toys, a pillow, a piggy bank, and a teddy bear. Reread the story and have the child act out what Maddie is doing. You can act out the part of the dad in the story and pretend to pick up the heavier objects.

• Show the child two objects (for example, a stuffed animal and a block) and have the child guess which of the two is heavier. Ask the child to explain his or her answer. Then have the child to pick up the objects to check the guess.

Following are some activities that will help you extend the concepts presented in *Mighty Maddie* into a child's everyday life:

**Balance Beam:** Have the child balance on one foot with arms out to the side. Give him or her a heavy object to hold in one hand. What happens to the child's balance? Which way does he or she fall? Ask the child why he or she thinks it is more difficult to keep his or her balance while holding a heavy object.

**Cleaning a Room:** Help the child make a cape with his or her name on the back. Then have the child act out the part of Mighty Maddie, cape and all, and clean his or her room. While picking up the room, have the child talk about which objects are heavy and which are light.

The following books include some of the same concepts that are presented in *Mighty Maddie*:

- THE DRAGON'S SCALES by Sarah Albee

- THE 100-POUND PROBLEM by Jennifer Dussling

- TELL ME HOW MUCH IT WEIGHS by Shirley Willis

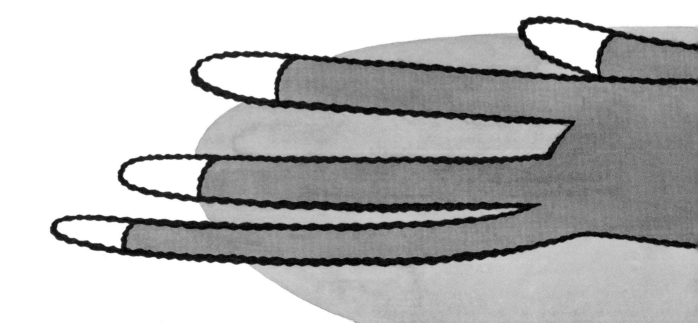